Mighty Mud Race

Written by Samantha Montgomerie

Illustrated by Pedro Riquelme

Collins

"Time to limber up," says Daddy as he laces up his sneakers.

Emmy touches her toes. "This is no time for an injury," she says. Dad nods.

Daddy is helping Emmy train for the Mighty Mud Race. There are five days to go.

Emmy taps her timer. “Ready, steady – go!” she says as she races off.

Emmy loves the steady thud of her feet when she races. Her body is strong.

"Sixty seconds quicker!" says Emmy.

Daddy wipes the sweat from his brow.
"Nice!" he says.

At dinner time, Emmy's tummy feels funny.
The next day is race day.

"You have done well training for this race," says Dad. "When you hit the mud, you will fly on through!"

Emmy cannot sleep. The Mighty Mud Race will be tricky. It's a long distance.

What if it's too muddy? What if she's clumsy and trips?

Emmy thinks of the race trail in her head as they drive to the race.

At the race line, Emmy spots her friend Min-Jun.
"Time to be mighty!" says Min-Jun, flapping his cape.

When the starter claps, Emmy whizzes off. She is ready to race!

"Go Emmy!" yells Dad. Daddy takes a photo on his phone.

Emmy waves as she sprints by.

Emmy keeps a steady pace as she curves by the pond. She peeks at her time and grins.

She takes a giant leap into the mud. It is thick and heavy.

Emmy treads through the thick gloopy mud. It is tricky – the mud is sloppy and slippery.

It is such grubby fun! Emmy looks back at Min-Jun. He's slipped over!

"Take my hand," says Emmy. Min-Jun winces.
She makes him steady.

They both finish, grubby and muddy.

"You are a mighty friend," says Min-Jun.

Mighty mud trail

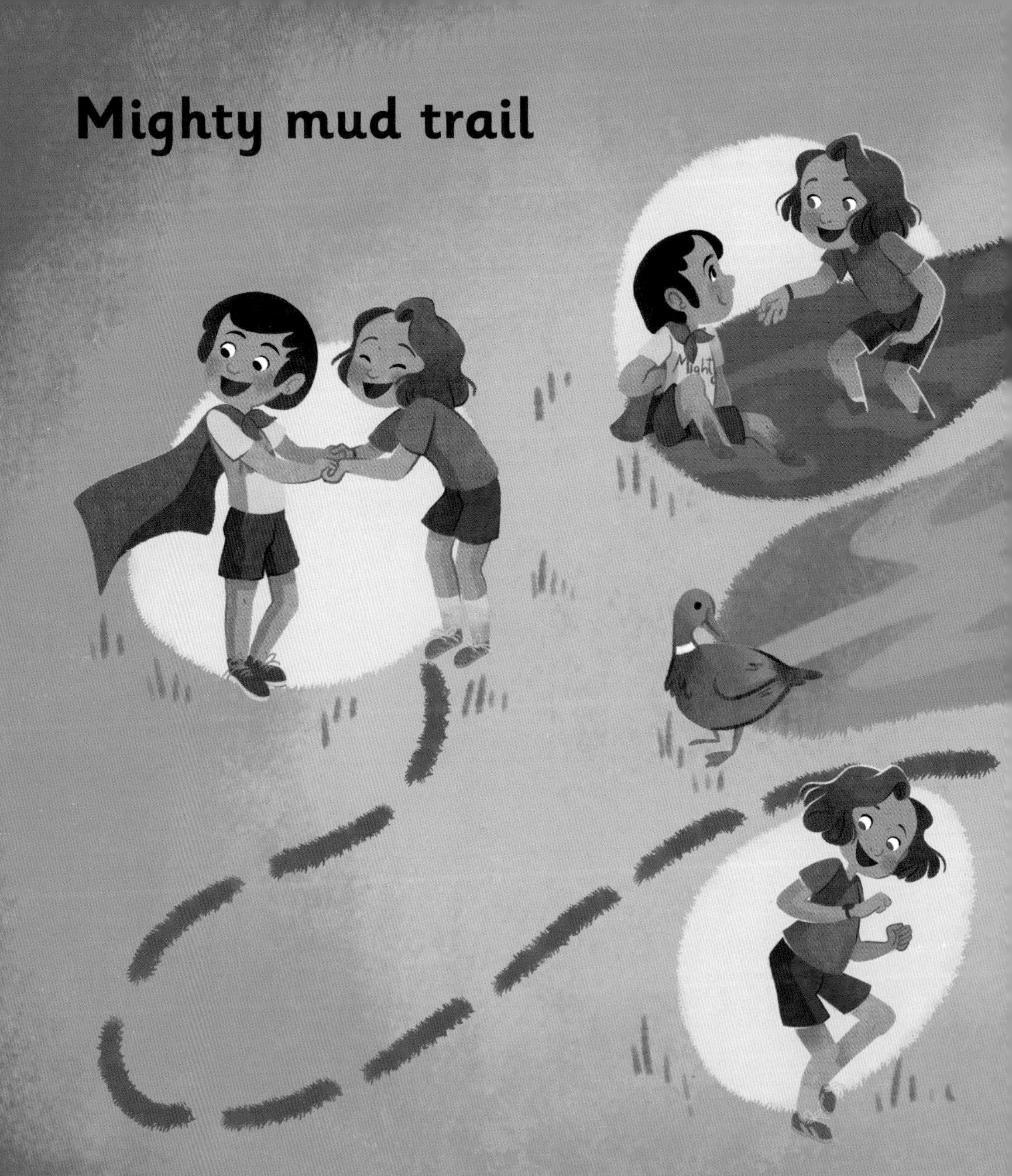

Review: After reading

Use your assessment from hearing the children read to choose any GPCs, words or tricky words that need additional practice.

Read 1: Decoding

- Discuss the meaning of **mighty** in context.
  - Discuss the title. Ask: Why is the race **Mighty**? Can the children think of any synonyms (words that mean the same or similar) to describe the race? (e.g. *big, tough, hard*)
  - Discuss what a **mighty friend** is on page 21. Ask: Why is Emmy a **mighty friend**? What synonym could be used instead? (e.g. *strong, important, extraordinary*)
- Challenge your child to identify the /e/ or /ee/ sounds in each of these words. Explain that some words might contain both sounds.

  steady **treads** **clumsy** **muddy** **ready** **sweat**
- Encourage the children to read page 2 or 3 to themselves, blending the words in their head and not out loud.

Read 2: Prosody

- Challenge children to use a change of pace to emphasise what happens as Emmy runs.
- Model reading page 16 speedily, to match her run. Then model reading page 17, slowing to a plodding pace for **It is thick and heavy**.
- Ask the children to read pages 16 and 17 to each other. Can they use a change of pace to show how the mud makes Emmy slow down?

Read 3: Comprehension

- Ask the children if they've ever been in a running race. Ask: What happened? Could you run fast or slow? Why?
- Look together at the end of the story, rereading pages 19 to 21.
  - Ask: Did Emmy win the race? Why? (*no, because she stopped to help Min-Jun*)
  - Talk about the theme of friendship and why Emmy is a **mighty friend**.
- Focus on the characters, settings and main event in the story.
  - Ask: Who are the main characters in the story? (*Emmy, Daddy, Dad and Min-Jun*)
  - Challenge the children to look through the book and list the different settings. (e.g. *garden, street, kitchen, bedroom, racetrack, finish line*)
  - Ask the children when in the story Emmy was most; nervous (e.g. *page 10 when she can't sleep*), excited (e.g. *page 15, when she sprints by*) and happy (*page 21, when she finishes with Min-Jun*). Ask: Why do you think that?
- Turn to pages 22 and 23 and ask children to talk about the mud race by using the pictures as prompts.